D1866798

LISTEN TO
BOB MARLEY

THE MAN
THE MUSIC
THE REVOLUTION

LISTEN TO BOB MARLEY

THE MAN THE MUSIC THE REVOLUTION

WORDS FROM
BOB MARLEY
SELECTED BY
CEDELLA MARLEY

OPEN ROAD
INTEGRATED MEDIA

TUFF GONG
BOOKS

CONTENTS

INTRODUCTION

This book was originally published as two volumes, created on the anniversaries of my dad's fifty-sixth and sixtieth Earthdays. In each volume, I selected some of my father's most prophetic poems and meditations, insights and conversational messages. I chose sayings that resonated with me and that were personally important to my dad as well. Within these books is a side of my father most people didn't get to see in his lifetime.

My father was always an explorer, an innovator, and a philosopher. He said, "Blessed reggae is a reggae when you deal with reality. You get more music, more anything." He always let his words and his music act as his messengers. He believed in unity and he expressed this philosophy in his music. He used his lyrics to connect people, to ask all of us to work together and trust one another. "We should all come together and create music and love," he said. If he had an opportunity to expand his message of freedom, religion, and social change, he embraced it.

My father still is truly an inspiration to so many. My family is livicated to making sure that his spirit thrives, along with the vibrancy of his music. We want his writings, his sense of the universe, his devotion to healing the world, and his endless charity to live on. My father passed quite young, and we did not get to spend the time with him that we wished—but from his music and his writings, we understand what he believed and we try to promote those teachings and philosophies. Today, his music and his legacy are still vital, so it is important to my family and me to keep his words alive in every way possible.

My dad said, "My music will go on forever. Maybe it's a fool to say that, but when me know facts me say facts. My music go on forever." He speaks the truth as always. . . .

—CEDELLA MARLEY

THE MAN

Since his passing thirty years ago Bob Marley's legend looms larger than ever, his life and music are unparalleled in their global popularity and depth of influence. Bob Marley was posthumously inducted into the Rock and Roll Hall of Fame in 1994; in December 1999 his 1977 album "Exodus" was named Album of the Century by Time Magazine and his song "One Love" was designated Song of the Millennium by the BBC. Marley's "Legend" compilation has annually sold over 250,000 copies since its release in 1984, according to Nielsen SoundScan, and it is only the 17th album to exceed sales of 10 million copies since SoundScan began its tabulations in 1991. These formidable achievements are all the more remarkable considering Bob's humble beginnings and the numerous challenges he endured trying to gain a foothold in Jamaica's chaotic music industry while skillfully navigating the politically partisan violence that abounded in Kingston, Jamaica throughout the 1970s.

One of the 20th century's most charismatic and challenging performers Marley's renown now transcends the role of reggae luminary: he is regarded as a cultural icon who implored his people to know their history "coming from the root of King David, through the line of Solomon," as he sang on "Blackman Redemption." Urging his listeners to check out the "Real Situation" and to rebel against the vampiric "Babylon System," Marley's lyrics continue to be mentally as well as physically liberating forces for Africans throughout the Diaspora and for oppressed peoples everywhere. "Bob had a rebel type of approach but his rebelliousness had a clearly defined purpose to it," acknowledges Chris Blackwell, the founder of Island Records, who played a pivotal role in introducing Marley and the Wailers to an international audience. "It wasn't just mindless rebelliousness, he was rebelling against the circumstances in which he and so many people found themselves."

EARLY YEARS

Born Nesta Robert Marley on February 6, 1945, to 50-year-old white quartermaster Captain Norval Marley, who was affiliated with the British West Indian Regiment and an eighteen-year-old black Jamaican woman, Cedella Malcolm Booker, Bob spent his early years in the rural community of Nine Miles. Located in the verdant parish of St. Ann, the residents of Nine Miles' have kept alive many traditions tied to the their African ancestry.

Norval and Cedella married in 1945 but Marley's family strongly disapproved of their union; although the Captain provided financial support, he seldom saw his son. The last time Nesta saw his father was when he took him to Kingston, supposedly to enroll him in school. Eighteen months later Cedella learned that Nesta wasn't attending school and was living with an elderly couple. Alarmed, she went to Kingston, searched, found Nesta and took him home to St. Ann.

In the late 1950s Bob, barely into his teens, left St. Ann with his mother and returned to Jamaica's capital. They eventually settled in a vicinity of western Kingston called Trench Town, so named because it was built over a sewage trench. A low-income, disenfranchised community comprised of government yards and squatter settlements Trench Town was nonetheless abundantly blessed with musical talent; Bob would later immortalize the area in his songs "No Woman No Cry" (1974), "Trench Town Rock" (1975) and "Trench Town" (released posthumously in 1983).

By the early 1960s the island's music industry was beginning to take shape and its development gave birth to an indigenous popular Jamaican music: ska. A local interpretation of American soul and R&B, with an irresistible accent on the offbeat, ska exerted a widespread influence on Jamaican youth. Music offered an escape from their otherwise harsh realities and the elusive lure of stardom was now a tangible goal within the burgeoning Jamaican music industry.

About this time, 16-year-old Bob Marley decided to embark on his dream of becoming a musician. While working as a welder Bob met aspiring singer Desmond Dekker, who would top the UK charts in a few years with his single "Israelites." Dekker introduced Marley to another young singer Jimmy Cliff the future star of the immortal Jamaican film "The Harder They Come." By age 14, Cliff had already recorded a couple of hit songs. In 1962 Cliff introduced Marley to producer Leslie Kong for whom he cut his first singles "Judge Not," "Terror" and "One More Cup of Coffee," a cover of the million selling country hit by Claude Gray. When these songs failed to connect with the public, Kong refused to pay Bob, an exploitative practice that was widespread during the infancy of Jamaica's music business.

EARLY
WAILERS

In 1964 Bob met Neville Livingston a.k.a. Bunny Wailer; together they began attending singing classes held by Trench Town resident Joe Higgs. There they met Peter (Macintosh) Tosh. The trio quickly became good friends and formed a vocal group The Wailing Wailers, with additional members Junior Braithwaite, Beverly Kelso, and Cherry Smith. Higgs assisted in the group's formation and gave them direction.

After just a couple recording sessions Smith and Braithwaite left the group and Kelso departed shortly thereafter. Bob, Bunny and Peter pressed on as a trio. They were introduced to Clement Sir Coxsone Dodd, founder of the seminal Jamaican label Studio One. The Wailers recorded several hits for Studio One including "Simmer Down," with Bob cautioning ghetto youths to control their tempers or "the battle would be harder." They attained a sizeable local following with their soulful harmonies, influenced primarily by American vocal group Curtis Mayfield and the Impressions, and lyrics that echoed the struggles facing poor Jamaican youths.

By the mid '60s the jaunty ska beat had metamorphosed into the slower paced rocksteady sound, which eventually gave way to Jamaica's signature reggae rhythm around 1968. Dodd had not made a corresponding shift in his label's releases nor did he embrace the Rastafarian imbued lyrics that came to the forefront as reggae developed. Declining sales of the Wailers' Studio One singles compounded by a lack of proper financial compensation from Dodd prompted their departure from Studio One.

Bob's mother relocated to the US state of Delaware and he spent a few months there in 1966. Upon his return to Jamaica, Bob and the Wailers established the Wail'N Soul'M label/record shop in front of his aunt's Trench Town home. The label's name identified its primary acts: The Wailers and The Soulettes, featuring Bob's wife, Rita. A few successful singles were released including "Bend Down Low" b/w "Mellow Mood" but due to lack of resources, the Wailers were forced to dissolve Wail'N Soul'M in 1968.

As the 1970s arrived, soaring unemployment, rationed food supplies, pervasive political violence and the IMF's stranglehold on the Jamaican economy due to various structural adjustment policies heavily influenced the social consciousness that came to define Bob's lyrics.

In 1970 the Wailers forged a crucial musical relationship with Jamaican producer Lee "Scratch" Perry, a pioneer in the development of dub. Perry wisely paired the vocalists with the nucleus of his studio band The Upsetters, brothers Aston "Family Man" and Carlton Barrett, playing bass and drums respectively. Collectively they forged a revolutionary sonic identity, as heard on tracks like "Duppy Conqueror," "400 Years" and "Soul Rebel," establishing an enduring paradigm for roots reggae. The Wailers' collaborations with Perry were featured on the albums "Soul Rebels" (1970) and "Soul Revolution" (1971).

Bob went to Sweden in 1971 to work with American singer Johnny Nash on a film score. He secured a contract with Nash's label CBS Records and by early 1972 The Wailers were in London promoting their single "Reggae On Broadway." When CBS abruptly abandoned the group there, Marley paid a chance visit to the offices of Island Records. The result was a meeting with label founder Chris Blackwell. Aware of the Wailers' formidable musical reputation, Blackwell advanced them £4,000 to record their next album, an unheard of sum to be given to a Jamaican act.

The Wailers' debut for Island Records "Catch A Fire" arrived in April 1973, and it garnered a great deal of (international) media fanfare. Tours of Britain and the US were quickly arranged. Bunny Wailer refused to participate in the US leg of the "Catch A Fire" tour and the Wailers' mentor Joe Higgs served as his replacement. Their US gigs included an opening slot for a then relatively unknown Bruce Springsteen in New York City and touring with Sly and the Family Stone, who were at their peak in the early 70s. The Wailers were removed from the Sly Stone tour after four dates because their riveting performances reportedly upstaged the headliner.

A second album for Island followed in October 1973; "Burnin" featured the timeless anthem of insurgency "Get Up Stand Up" and "I Shot The Sheriff," which Eric Clapton covered and took to the top of the Billboard Hot 100 in 1974, the same year that Peter Tosh and Bunny Wailer exited the group.

m

BOB MARLEY
AND THE WAILERS

Bob's third Island Records release "Natty Dread" was credited to Bob Marley and The Wailers. Peter and Bunny's harmonizing was replaced with the soulfulness of the I-Threes (Rita Marley, Marcia Griffiths and Judy Mowatt). The Wailers band now included Family Man and Carly Barrett, Junior Marvin and Al Anderson on lead guitar, Tyron Downie and Earl "Wya" Lindo on keyboards and Alvin "Seeco" Patterson playing percussion. "Natty Dread" cracked the top 100 in the US and the UK. It featured the poignant "No Woman No Cry," and the defining title track, which played a significant role in introducing Rastafarian culture and philosophies to the world.

"Bob Marley and the Wailers Live" followed, capturing a thrilling performance at London's Lyceum Ballroom during the "Natty Dread" tour. That album's melancholy version of "No Woman No Cry" reached the UK top 40.

Bob catapulted to international stardom in 1976 with the release of "Rastaman Vibration," which peaked at number 8 on the Billboard Top 200. With songs like "Crazy Baldhead" and the stirring title track "Rastaman Vibration" presented a clearer understanding of Rastafari teachings to the mainstream audience that was now attentively listening to Bob. Also included was "War," its lyrics taken from an impassioned speech to the United Nations General Assembly in 1963 delivered by Ethiopian Emperor and Rastafarian Deity Haile Selassie. Thirty-five years later "War" remains an unassailable anthem of equality, its empowering spirit embraced by dispossessed people everywhere.

As 1976 drew to a close Bob was now a global ambassador for Rastafari, a distinction that fostered an immense sense of pride among many Jamaicans, especially the ghetto dwellers for whom his messages carried the greatest significance. But Bob's pervasive influence was also a point of contention for others within a country bitterly and too often bloodily divided by politics. In early December 1976 Bob was scheduled to headline Smile Jamaica, a free concert held in Kingston with the aim of suppressing the simmering political tensions between Jamaica's rival People's National Party (PNP) and the Jamaica Label Party (JLP). The day before, an unsuccessful murder attempt was made on his life at his Kingston home. Bob and Rita were left with minor gun shot wounds while manager Don Taylor and friend Lewis Griffith were seriously injured. Bob defiantly performed at Smile Jamaica but within minutes of leaving the concert, he was on a plane en route to the UK.

Bob lived in London for the next 18 months where he recorded the albums "Exodus" (1977) and "Kaya" (1978). Exodus remained on the UK charts for a staggering 56 consecutive weeks. It spawned three popular singles "Exodus," "Waiting In Vain" and Bob's first British top 10 hit "Jammin." In a more romantic vein, the "Kaya" album hit number 4 on the British charts, propelled by the popularity of the singles "Satisfy My Soul" and "Is This Love?"

In April 1978 Bob returned to Jamaica to perform at the One Love Peace Concert, another attempt at curtailing the rampant violence stemming the senseless PNP and the JLP rivalries. In a daring, dramatic gesture, Bob summoned JLP leader Edward Seaga and Prime Minister Michael Manley onstage. As the Wailers pumped out the rhythm to "Jammin," Bob urged the politicians to shake hands; clasping his left hand over theirs, he raised their arms aloft and chanted "Jah Rastafari." In recognition of his courageous attempt to bridge Jamaica's brutal, cavernous political divide, Bob traveled to the United Nations in New York on June 6, 1978 where he received the organization's Medal of Peace.

At the end of 1978 Bob made his first trip to Africa, visiting Kenya and then Ethiopia, the spiritual home of Rastafari. Earlier Wailers' tours of Europe and America were featured on their second live album "Babylon By Bus." That same year Bob and The Wailers toured Japan, Australia and New Zealand, where the indigenous Maori people greeted them with a traditional welcoming ceremony typically reserved for visiting dignitaries.

Bob released his ninth album for Island, "Survival" in the summer of 1979. An inspiring, politically progressive work championing pan-African solidarity, "Survival" included "Africa Unite" and "Zimbabwe." The latter was an anthem for the soon to be liberated colony of Rhodesia. In April 1980 Bob and the Wailers performed at Zimbabwe's official Independence Ceremony at the invitation of the country's newly elected president Robert Mugabe. This profound honor was further confirmation of Bob Marley and the Wailers' importance throughout the African Diaspora and reggae's significance as a unifying and liberating force.

"Uprising" the final album to be released in Bob's lifetime helped to fulfill another career objective. Bob had openly courted an African American listenership throughout his career and he made a profound connection with that demographic through the danceable single "Could You Be Loved," which has become a mainstay on urban radio formats. "Uprising" also included the acoustic "Redemption Song" a declaration of enduring truths and profoundly personal reflections; Angelique Kidjo, the Clash's Joe Strummer, Sinead O'Connor and Rihanna are but four of the dozens of artists who have recorded versions "Redemption Song."

Bob Marley and The Wailers embarked on a major European tour in the spring of 1980, breaking attendance records in several countries. In Milan, Italy, they performed before 100,000 people, the largest audience of their career. The US leg of the "Uprising" tour commenced in Boston on September 16 at the JB Hynes Auditorium. On September 19 Bob and the Wailers rolled into New York City for two consecutive sold out nights at Madison Square Garden as part of a bill featuring New York based rapper Kurtis Blow and Lionel Richie and the Commodores. The tour went onto the Stanley Theater in Pittsburgh, Pa. where Bob delivered the final set of his illustrious career, on September 23, 1980.

The Pittsburgh show took place just two days after Marley learned that the cancer that had taken root in his big toe in 1977, following a football injury, had metastasized and spread throughout his body. Bob courageously fought the disease for eight months, even traveling to Germany to undergo treatment at the clinic of Dr. Josef Issels. At the beginning of May 1981, Bob left Germany to return to Jamaica but he did not complete that journey, succumbing to his cancer in a Miami hospital in May 11, 1981.

In April 1981 Bob Marley was awarded Jamaica's third highest honor, the Order of Merit, for his outstanding contribution to his country's culture. Ten days after he passed away, the Honorable Robert Nesta Marley O.M. was given a state funeral by the Jamaican government, attended by Prime Minister Edward Seaga and the Opposition Party Leader Michael Manley. Hundreds of thousands of spectators lined the streets to observe the procession of cars that wound its way from Kingston to Bob's final resting place, a mausoleum in his birthplace of Nine Miles. Thirty years on, Bob Marley's music remains as vital as ever in its celebration of life and embodiment of struggle.

MARLEY'S GLOBAL LEGACY

As the most important singer/songwriter of the 20th century Bob Marley has exerted an unparalleled influence among disparate populations throughout the world. New Zealand's indigenous Maori people, for example, greeted Bob with a traditional song and dance ceremony reserved for visiting dignitaries when he arrived in their country for a concert at Auckland's Westeren Springs Stadium on April 6, 1979. Marley's former manager, the late Don Taylor, referred to the Maori welcoming ritual as "one of my most treasured memories of the impact of Bob and reggae music on the world." On April 17, 1980 when the former British colony Rhodesia was officially renamed Zimbabwe and the Union Jack replaced with the red, gold, green and black Zimbabwean flag, it is said that the first words officially spoken in the new nation were "ladies and gentlemen, Bob Marley and the Wailers." Zimbabwean freedom fighters in their ongoing struggle to end minority rule were strengthened by Marley's empowering lyrics. Marley had penned a tribute to their efforts, "Zimbabwe," which was included on the most overtly political album of his career, 1979's "Survival" and he was invited to headline their official liberation celebrations. Zimbabwean police used teargas to control the crowds that surged through the gates of Harare's Rufaro Stadium to get a glimpse of

Marley onstage. As several members of his entourage fled for cover, Marley, returned to the stage to perform "Zimbabwe," the power of his words ringing with a greater urgency amidst the ensuing chaos: *"to divide and rule could only tear us apart, in everyman chest, mm—there beats a heart/so soon we'll find out who is the real revolutionaries and I don't want my people to be tricked by mercenaries.* "There was smoke everywhere, our eyes filled with tears so we ran off," recalls Marcia Griffiths, who sang back up for Marley, alongside his wife Rita Marley and Judy Mowatt, as the I-Threes. "When Bob saw us the next day he smiled and said now we know who are the real revolutionaries."

A generation later a group of political refugees from Sierra Leone living in Guinean concentration camps, traumatized by years of bloody warfare in their country, found strength through Marley's music, which inspired them to form a band and write/record their own songs. The Refugee All Stars won international acclaim for their 2006 debut "Living Like A Refugee" and their 2010 album "Rise and Shine," each utilizing an amalgam of reggae, Sierra Leone's Islamic rooted *bubu* music and West African *goombay.*

On October 13, 2010, Victor Zamora, one of 33 Chilean miners rescued after being trapped in a San Jose mine for 69 days, asked to hear Marley's "Buffalo Soldier" upon his release. Recorded in 1980 and released in 1983 "Buffalo Soldier" recounts the atrocities of the slave trade and like so many of Marley's songs, it highlights the importance of relating past occurrences to present-day identities *"if you know your history then you will know where you are coming from, then you wouldn't have to ask me, who the hell do I think I am?"*

BOB AND
RASTAFARI

Marley's own multifaceted identity represents progressive political ideologies, a revered pan-African consciousness and deep spiritual convictions, each derived from his firmly rooted commitment to the Rastafarian way of life. "The combination of his own inquisitiveness and the profound depth and influence of the Rastafari movement helped to lift Bob Marley from being just another entertainer and made him into a transformative artist that reshaped not only reggae music but also the course of world history," says Carlyle McKetty, President of the Brooklyn, NY based Coalition to Preserve Reggae Music. "The intricate relationship between reggae and Rasta is seminal to understanding and preserving the reggae form and Bob Marley's keen understanding and internalization of the tenets of the Rastafari movement have yet to be adequately explored."

The Rastafari movement has been referenced in Jamaican popular music since the early 60s and by the late 70s its principles had come to define roots reggae's lyrical content. It was Marley who introduced Rastafari to an international audience through his 1970s' Island Record releases including "Catch A Fire" and "Burnin'" (both recorded with Tosh and Wailer and released in 1973) and subsequent albums with the Wailers band featuring brothers Aston and Carlton Barrett, on bass and drums respectively. "Natty Dread" (1974) was the first Marley album to chart in the US; "Rastaman Vibration" Marley's highest US charting album (at no. 8) rightfully proclaimed Rasta as offering *"a new time, a new day"* on its title track. Released in 1976, "Rastaman Vibration" also included "War" a stirring equality anthem, its lyrics taken from an address to the United Nations' General Assembly in 1963 by Ethiopian Emperor His Imperial Majesty Haile Selassie I, who is considered a living God among Rastafarians. "War's" globally pertinent lyrics *("until the color of a man's skin is of no more significance than the color of his eyes . . . until the ignoble and unhappy regime that holds our brothers in Angola, in Mozambique, in South Africa, in subhuman bondage, have been toppled and utterly destroyed everywhere is war")* and the reverence with which Marley regarded His Majesty's words transformed his performances of the song into spellbinding displays, as seen at concerts in Milan, Italy, where he performed before a crowd of 100,000, the largest audience of his career, to New York City's prestigious Madison Square Garden, which he sold out for two consecutive nights, to the Stanley Theater, in Pittsburgh, PA, where he delivered the final set of his illustrious career, on September 23, 1980. The Pittsburgh show took place just two days after Marley learned that the cancer that had taken root in his big toe in 1977 had now spread throughout his body. A committed revolutionary, Marley delivered a career defining set in Pittsburgh, which included a haunting acoustic rendition of "Redemption Song," from "Uprising" (1980), the final album released during his lifetime.

—PATRICIA MESCHINO

THE MUSIC

LIVICATION

Let the words of our mouth

and the meditation of our hearts

be acceptable in thy sight,

O Far I.

—CEDELLA

CONTENTS

INTRODUCTION

Recently my children have been asking about their grandfather, and so I have written *The Boy from Nine Miles: The Early Life of Bob Marley* and now *56 Thoughts from 56 Hope Road*. This book of meditations is really like having a conversation with my dad. These are his thoughts. They are not songs—what comes out here is raw and real. And it's a personal side very few people get to see.

Music is what it is . . . people attach themselves to it in a certain way. The spoken word is a different kind of reality. Like when he said, "Me live in the world but I'm not of the world." From that, you could say, what is going on in the world is not really for you. Because, really, you create your own world, your own safety and sanctity. And when my dad said, "I did not come to bow, I came to conquer," I think of how I am raising my own children right now. I refuse to lie. I refuse to tell my kids to believe in tooth fairies, Halloween, Columbus Day. I tell my children, Chris Columbus didn't discover Jamaica. He was the Tourist Board. So, by telling the truth about things, you are not bowing; you are conquering.

My father is such a strong presence. But we are all extensions of someone we're related to, and not related to, and that is the strong presence in us. When I do things for the benefit of my brothers and sisters, I become my father. And whether I am building an empire, physical or spiritual, I am doing it for my father. When he said,

"How could you deny me my simplicity?" I think he was aware that even with all that he had accomplished, he had the right to make that statement. In truth, he didn't call himself anything. He was just who he was. Often he worked only for others. So they would have food to eat. And when he said to us, "You have no friends," what he really meant was that we had many brothers and sisters. Daddy was one man but he left an army. I think the most important thing he taught me was that nobody is beyond redemption. Nobody. He said, too, that envy is the number one killer of man. Well, my father had so much to say. Hopefully, these 56 thoughts will help you to stay upful and right.

—CEDELLA MARLEY

SONG

1

If god didn't want me to sing,
I wouldn't have a song to sing.

2

Bend down low
Let me tell you
What I know.
Fisherman row,
You're going to reap
What you sow.

3

One good thing about music,
When it hits you feel no pain.

4

Say you just can't live
That negative way,
If you know what I mean,
Make way for that positive day.

5

Sun is shining
The weather is sweet.
Makes you want to move
Your dancing feet.

6

Hey, mister music
Sure sounds good to me.
I can't refuse it,
What to be got to be.

7

There's a natural mystic
Blowing through the air.
If you listen carefully now,
You will hear . . .
Many more will have to suffer,
Many more will have to die,
Don't ask me why.

LIFE

8

Me don't love fighting,
But me don't love wicked either . . .
I guess I have a kinda war thing in me.
But is better to die fighting for freedom
Than to be a prisoner
All the days of your life.

9

I know I was
Born with a price on my head.

10

Jamaica is a place where
You build up competition in your mind.
We should all come together and
Create music and love.

11

How long shall
They kill our prophets
While we stand aside
And look?
Some say it's just
A part of it,
We have to fulfill the book.

12

And whosoever diggeth a pit
Shall fall in it.
Whosoever diggeth a pit
Shall bury in it.

13

Trodding through creation
In a irie meditation.

14

The road of life is rocky
And you may stumble, too.
So while you point your finger
Someone else is judging you.

LOVE

15

Children is wonderful,
a part of my richness.

16

Oh let Jah love
Come shining in
Into our lives again.

17

The rain is falling,
And I just can't stop calling . . .
And I just can't tell the raindrops
From my teardrops
That's falling on my face.

18

Woman is to be loved
and appreciated.
Woman is an earth,
the mother of creation.
Must love woman,
but don't fall in love.
Me stand in love.
Love so much me look hungry.

19

I want to love you
And treat you right.
I want to love you
Every day and every night.
We'll be together with a roof
Right over our heads.
We'll share the shelter
Of my single bed.
We'll share the same room,
Jah provide the bread.

20

One love, one heart.
Let's get together and feel all right.
As it was in the beginning,
So it shall be in the end.

21

All you got to do
Is give a little,
Take a little.

WORLD

22

Me not of the world, y'know.
Me live in the world but
I'm not of the world.

23

Me mustn't fight for my rights,
My rights must come to me.

24

I don't come to bow,
I come to conquer.

25

If you get up and quarrel
Every day, you're saying
Prayers to the devil, I say.

26

Overcome
The devils
With
A thing
Named
Love.

27

What we really want
Is the right to be right
And the right to be wrong.

28

The most intelligent people
Is the poorest people.
Yes, the thief them rich,
Pure robbers and thieves, rich!
The intelligent and innocent are poor,
Are crumbled and get brutalized. Daily.

WAR

29

In the beginning
Jah created everything.
He gave man dominion
Over all things.
But now it's too late,
You see, men have lost
Their faith
Eating up all the flesh
From off the earth.

30

Two thousand years of history
Could not be wiped away so easily.

31

We no know how
We and them
a-go work it out.
But someone will have to pay
For the innocent blood
That they shed
Every day
It's what the Bible say.

32

Destruction of the poor
Is the poverty.
Destruction of the soul
Is vanity.

33

There should be no war
between black and white!
But until white people listen to
black people with open ears,
there must be—well—suspicion.

34

How many rivers do we have to cross
Before we can talk to the boss?
All that we've gained we've lost.
We must've really paid the cost.

35

Would you let the system
Make you kill your brother man?
Would you make the system
Get on top of your head again?

36

Check out the real situation,
Nation war against nation.
Where did it all begin?
Where will it end?
Well, it seems like total destruction
Is the only solution.

JAH

37

Take Jah sun
And Jah moon
And Jah rain
And Jah stars
And forever erase
Your fantasy.

38

Zion train is coming our way.

39

Every thing in life has its purpose,
Find its reason,
In every season . . .
We'll be forever loving Jah.

40

Once a man
And twice a child,
And everything
Is just for a while.

41

Jah appear to me in a vision
So sweet: it's me brother,
Me father, me mother, me creator,
Everything.

42

Selassie-I,
You can check him so.
Morning, him a baby.
Today, him a bird.
Jah live!

JOURNEY

43

My music will go on forever.
Maybe it's a fool say that,
But when me know
Facts me can say facts.
My music go on forever.

44

What is my message?
Truth, peace and love
And music and livity.

45

Why do you look so sad
And forsaken?
When one door is closed
Don't you know
Another is open?

46

Life, it's life we deal with . . .
He that sees the light
And knows the light
Shall live.

47

One of my good friends said,
In a reggae riddim,
Don't jump in the water
if you can't swim . . .

48

There is one mystery
I just can't express.
How can you ever
Give your more
To receive your less?

49

Don't let them change you
Or even rearrange you.

50

Though my days
Are filled with sorrow,
I see there a bright tomorrow.

HOME

51

Bob Marley isn't my name,
I don't even know my name yet.

52

My home is in my head.

53

It's a foolish dog
Bark at a flying bird.
One preacher must learn
To respect the shepherd.

54

In high seas
Or low seas,
I'm gonna be your friend.

55

When the morning
Gathers the rainbow
Want you to know
I'm a rainbow, too.

56

I've been here before
And will come again.

THE REVOLUTION

LIVICATION

Let the words of our mouth

and the meditation of our hearts

be acceptable in thy sight,

O Far I.

CONTENTS

FOREWORD
& FORWARD

This is not just a book we are bringing out, turning out, releasing or re-releasing. This is a book that is already on the breath of the air. It's a book already released, and well alive.

Why 60 visions?

Well, my father is sixty years young now. His life force moves many, and the many move mountains. We hold these prophecies to be timeless, yet so timely.

What my father said is as fresh as the day. "Jah create all a we. So is the same breath which is I." My father lives in these words. Breathe them in, let them go.

Sixty and still smokin'!

—CEDELLA MARLEY

BOOK I
JUDGMENT DAYS

1

My heart can be hard as stone and soft as water.

These days are the judgment days, only the fittest of the fittest shall survive.

2

If you don't know God you gonna suffer and dead.

I could starve and suffer too, but I know Jah.

3

The point is the fulfillment of Revelation. I no say is my work to go out in a Babylon to really do what I do, but I find myself doing it, and I cannot stop it because a greater power than the power of I know of myself, make I do it.

4

I personally is a servant of His Imperial Majesty doing no hard work, just doing what Jah say I have to do. And true, him give I the power to play music and him give I the inspiration to say these things to the people who Him work through. Because I know say, Jah have I and I living in every life.

5

I mean maybe it's the beginning. You know, me live within the time, and me know what a gwaan. Because it's the consciousness against folly; that's the Armageddon. Now, you know, you could have war, big war, and them thing there, but I and I prepare to meet Jah, while other people prepare for war, because is when them destroy themselves, is not really righteous people like to fight bloody battles. We prepare to meet our God . . . who not prepare to meet God? Them fight the war. Is war them deal with, so them must kill themselves.

6

A planned revolution you can get hurt. The only control you can have is if Jah really love you, and him take you from the revolution. Is the whole universe involved in this revolution. Dangerous things happen like in them earthquake, all them things come up in the revolution. A long shaking for five minutes. All I know is, the time is now. If you can go through all them things and still be alive, you can live; you must be special.

7

Every time I plant a seed, he say kill it before it grow. Just imagine what really a gwaan. A dangerous thing. Fighting against people; that is not me. People fight against themselves.

8

Now, some people are devil and some people are angel. Jah say leave all judgment unto Him. Is certain things a man have to really keep to himself because you can say things, at the time you say it; it not so right. These are what Jah teach you every day and sometimes you have to learn, you have to know what Him say.

9

Started out crying, you know, and then music becomes a part, or is a part, or was a part. Is really a thing what me have to think about because me can't be ungrateful to Jah, because today we start, yet it was yesterday, you know. So, from the beginning Jah did created it inna the starting for the man to start. So me really have to think about from Creation then.

SHC

10

Rastafari live, you know. As I would say, Jah live I-tinually, and there's a natural mystic blowing through the air.

BOOK II
TRIBULATIONS

11

This morning I woke up in a curfew. Oh, God, I was a prisoner too. Could not recognize the faces standing over me, they were all dressed in uniforms of brutality . . . Is not really literally about burning down the city. It's about burning certain things out of our mind to live in harmony.

12

So much people have to die to make the other people not even live but see the mistake that those that die make.

13

I know say people live off false pretense . . . the majority of them . . . and I know say, I and I don't have to suffer the way others suffer, not because of material things, but in some way, material things become an object where I and I have to suffer.

14

If me want, me no really crave. Can't want. Because where me grow, me know everything you could want. Stones was my toys and trees and bush and flowers. They were my toys. So I don't grow up and want things. Is millions of stones used to be round me, and me used to go play amongst the flowers them, and play as a little youth; and so me grow up loving the hills more than the things of want. Because want is just the things you want that people make; so I really want nothing.

15

We don't think upon a low level. We think high. That means we can live and we can see things. We can stay from above, and see things low. If you stay from below and look above, you have want. If you stay from above and look 'pon them below, then you can't want. Because you have to bend down too low to pick up something.

16

And true, the people and the teaching what them get, them want to come teach me the same teaching. The old wine what them get. We show them the truth today, and so them fight against the truth because of self-pride and respect. Because you're older than me I shouldn't come tell you something; it's the truth, and sometimes it have to bust out of you like river.

17

My music fight against the system that teaches to live and die.

18

Is only opportunists a go through tribulations right now. Because tribulations 'pon both side; for the youth when them come and the man when him get old.

19

Laws cause crime and violence. Earth a come, earth a forward to creation. All the laws that we abide by are blah-blah and boom-boom-boom because we have to suffer, as any man can know that. The laws we have no must be a must. The only law which is law is the law of life. The law how to live.

20

A man build him a city and say him want them to run it. And these people to live yah so. Me no want to talk like a politician; me just want to talk about righteousness. Like say, Jah is earth rightful ruler. And him don't run no wire fence.

21

You can just imagine if everyone on earth did have one day where we just put all our minds together regardless where the force is, as long as it's positive, and just meditate for even a hour that day. And just live nice with them nice meditation. I mean, now, the climate would be nice, the smog would a leave.

BOOK III
WAKE UP AND LIVE

22

Anyone who cry out for justice is a Wailer.

23

Money doesn't matter. Only music matters. When people think first about the money and then about the music the music won't be worth the money they were thinking about.

24

Music is the biggest gun, because it save. It nuh kill, right? The other gun lick off your head!

25

Is not the people we come to play . . . we come to play music.

26

And there shall be sheep and wolf in sheep clothing. But I and I couldn't watch that this day. Because I and I have to live Rasta and know Rasta. And I no come to judge a man; Jah say leave all judgment unto Him.

27

One time I felt like I should take up my arms and do a thing. But Jah say, No youth, cool, because a so this earth rest. And I glad say, that's how it work out for I man . . . too much wickedness out there, you know.

28

Well, I say many shall be called but only few chosen. And then the people have to listen to the trumpet, which is not no trumpet come a blow, but is a man a go talk, His Imperial Majesty, Earth Rightful Ruler.

29

Sometimes, you know, it come out with "we" and "me," but you consciously want to know something, them can tell you, "I." Jah create all a we. So is the same breath which is I; I and I.

30

The god who make I and I, him create technicolor people.

31

My music defends righteousness. If you're black and you're wrong, you're wrong; if you're white and you're wrong, you're wrong; if you're Indian and you're wrong, you're wrong. It's universal.

32

Blessed reggae is a reggae when you deal with reality. You get more music, more anything. You feel dirt, the earth. You feel it, different from just thinking about it.

33

You change if you change from Babylon to Rasta, but you can't change from Rasta to anything. When the truth awaken in you, you can't do anything but accept the truth.

34

So Jah say, not one of my seeds shall sit on the sidewalk and beg your bread.

35

Prejudice is a chain, it can hold you. If you prejudice, you can't move, you keep prejudice for years. Never get nowhere with that.

36

Give a man a chance, you know? I don't want to crucify a man like they crucified Christ, just because he wasn't a Rastaman.

BOOK IV
VISION

37

Me dream some melodies. But when you wake up you can't hear them. Inspiration come from vision. Young man say dream; old man say vision. Any time something happen Jah show me the vision. Whenever anything that might affect me, Jah show me before it happen.

38

I no do this thing for money business. This thing is as if Jah come in a I heart. And make it move.

39

Be still and know that His Imperial Majesty, Emperor Haile Selassie I of Ethiopia is the Almighty. Now the Bible say so. Babylon newspaper say so. And I and I, the children, say so. I don't see what our people want more God to reveal to them. What them want? Them want a white God? Well, God come black.

40

You know, me can always do what me want to do. Just in time, everything happen in time. You see, God is my father and him grow me just the way a son suppose to be grown. The perfect father for me.

41

We are revolutionaries fighting single-handed with music.

42

I don't think about power. Funny word. God, he has the power and he has not stopped working.

43

Music is a thing that grow. Is an earth feeling, music. Earth feeling music. E-A-R-T-H. So you know people must feel it. The whole thing, maybe, is not me understanding what is to be said; but having something to say.

44

My life here, this flesh; me have to live, me never say there was no fear of death but me no deal with death. Me have no time to risk this flesh too much 'cause it's this me have to do it in.

45

Me is a natural man like any other man, and me feel like any other man. I don't really feel like an entertainer or a star or any of them thing there. Me know what me want, me know where me come from, and me know where me go.

46

I don't have a religion, you know. This is what I am. I am a Rastaman; so this is not religion. This is life.

47

Rasta is the future. Seen? Rasta is the future, still.

48

Unity is the world's key, and racial harmony. Until the white man stops calling himself white and the black man stops calling himself black, we will not see it. All the people on earth are just one family.

49

My music must be a gift. Some people call everything a gift. It's a reality. The work just comes so you have to do it. This God do all things, you know what I mean? So me personally as a man is nothing without the inspiration of Jah.

50

The father have three sons: Ham, Shem and Japhet. Japhet him get wisdom of technology. We need technology, in a sense. Is no way you can walk this earth; this earth not like it was in the beginning. Now you really have to cross a vast amount of water. Development is not a problem; it is the flesh. The man himself is him own problem. Seen?

51

I man a farmer since creation.

52

When you smoke herb, herb reveal itself to you. All the wickedness you do, herb will reveal to your conscience; herb will show up yourself clear, see yourself through. Herb make you meditate.

53

Herb make you live with people good, you know. You just have to live with people good because it tell you when you smoke it, it directly show you. It's love. It's love in me . . . meditation upon God, you know . . . It's like people use herb for any direction they want to go . . . I mean, if a guy smoke herb him could be a bad guy, him meditate on how to be bad . . . And if you smoke it to be good, it show you how it is to be good.

54

Everybody eat beef. You can have more tender meaning toward a cow. The cow give milk. I mean, should not really kill the cow to eat the cow. Because I feel them can drink the milk and then you have other things that you can eat to get the same things like meat protein have . . . I don't exactly like big dead flesh in front of me.

55

When is music time, me serious. Just so me stay, we no in a joke business.

56

Babylon no want peace, man. Babylon want power.

57

Music is a dangerous game. A musician man is a man him soft in him heart. Him slightly different.

58

Our children is born in our spirit, so you can't teach them, you can only enlighten them . . . you can't really tell them anything because them done come from a place where them learn truth already, and them hear that truth when them was babies.

59

Your belly's full but we're hungry for the love of our brethren. Food might be in your belly, but there's more to living than just filling it.

Where's the love of your brother?

60

When you rest at night-time you put your head down and go to sleep. Where yourself is at that time?

. . . yet you wake again . . .

A BIOGRAPHY OF
CEDELLA MARLEY

As the first born of Bob and Rita Marley, Cedella Marley is a descendant of reggae royalty; as an accomplished singer, an inspiring author, an adventurous designer, and a visionary entrepreneur, she is also a self-made woman, with each aspect of her multifaceted creativity honoring her exalted familial legacy.

Born on August 23, 1967, the world met Cedella as a singing and dancing teenager with The Melody Makers, the Marley sibling group featuring her younger brothers Ziggy on lead vocals and guitar and Stephen on percussion and vocals. For two decades The Melody Makers toured the world establishing a new generation of Marley musical mystique, as they sold millions of albums and reaped an assortment of prestigious honors including three Grammy Awards.

Cedella balanced the Melody Makers' rigorous touring schedule with the responsibilities of motherhood (she and her husband have three sons), the management of the Marley family's numerous business endeavors and the demands of designing her (celebrated) women's casual wear collection Catch A Fire, named after her father's first album for Island Records. She is the CEO of Tuff Gong International, the record label founded by her father in 1965 and director of The Bob Marley Foundation, a not for profit charitable organization. She is the overseer of Marley and Company, a Marley family entity that manages the rights to Bob's name and likeness, and the Marley merchandising conglomerate House of Marley. Cedella also helms 1Love.org the family's recently launched social networking/charity website. When family members realized Bob Marley's Facebook page had more than 18 million "friends," they decided to channel all of that energy into something positive. 1Love.org has partnered with the United Nations Environment Program and charity: water, a nonprofit initiative that brings clean and safe drinking water to people in developing countries, to direct fans to charitable organizations and causes important to the Marley family. "Dad's message and vision of "One Love" is as relevant today as it was 30 years ago," says Cedella, "now we can use social media to spread the message and put his words into reality."

As director of the Bob Marley Foundation, Cedella supervises a range of programs that provide financial assistance and other resources to various institutions, including Kingston's Bustamante Children's Hospital and Victoria Jubilee Hospital (where Cedella was born); the Stepney Primary and Junior High (Bob's former school in St. Ann, Jamaica) and the Eira Schrader Golden Age Home located in the west Kingston community of Trenchtown where Bob was raised and later immortalized in the reggae classics "Trenchtown Rock" and "No Woman No Cry." Some of the Foundation's current projects include rewarding scholarships/fellowships qualified individuals to attend academic and/or trade institutions in the Caribbean and Africa, as well as continuing education classes, seminars and workshops presented by professionals in the arts, entertainment, music, and sports industries, with the aim of increasing employment opportunities.

In 1993 Cedella was appointed as C.E.O. of Tuff Gong International and she has played a pivotal role in the expansion of its operations. The Tuff Gong group of companies now includes a renowned state of the art recording studio in Kingston, Jamaica, which is utilized by the island's top reggae artists and producers, Marley's sons, and an array of international artists including Senegalese superstar Youssou N'Dour who recorded "Dakar-Kingston," his 2010 Marley tribute album there. Tuff Gong also houses a (vinyl) record and CD manufacturing plant, an analog and digital mastering room, a worldwide distribution network, a wholesale and retail record outlet, even a book division.

Cedella also supervises the licensing of her father's image and approves all artwork for The House of Marley, a joint venture launched in mid 2010 with HoMedics, the leading global manufacturer of home massage, relaxation, and wellness products. The initial items from the House of Marley include boomboxes, iPod docking stations, ear buds and headphones, each accented with the Rastafarian colors of red, green and gold. The House of Marley will soon roll out additional eco-friendly products utilizing woods, bamboo, recycled materials, and reduced-waste packaging, all inspired by Bob's music and the oneness philosophy heard in his lyrics.

"We have been diligent about protecting our father's legacy over the years," stated Cedella. "There is enormous demand for products that allow his legend to live on and this partnership allows us to grow his legacy, while maintaining his integrity and artistic DNA in a quality manner." House of Marley will also expand existing Marley brands including Cedella's Catch A Fire clothing collection, which debuted to rave reviews in 2001. Presenting tailored, bohemian-chic jackets, jeans, accessories and an assortment of tees, Catch A Fire has been featured in numerous top fashion publications including *Vogue* and *Women's Wear Daily.* The line is carried in major department stores including Nordstrom, Neiman Marcus and Saks Fifth Avenue as well as numerous upscale boutiques.

Cedella is currently designing additional collections for the Marley family's apparel company Zion Rootswear, including a deconstructed children's clothing line, "Nice Time," and a menswear line.

Cedella is also an accomplished children's book author, having written *The Boy from Nine Miles (The Early Life of Bob Marley)* and *Three Little Birds,* a vividly illustrated story based on her father's song of the same name, both published by Tuff Gong Books. Scheduled for publication by Chronicle Books in the fall of 2011 is Cedella's "One Love," its storyline adapted from the lyrics to her father's beloved song, which was designated as the Song of the Century by the BBC.

As if all of that weren't enough to keep her busy, Cedella continues to record. Her latest single "Can You Feel the Love Tonight" from The Lion King, was included on the 2010 release "The Disney Reggae Club," a compilation of famous songs sung by reggae artists (including her brother Ziggy) with the intention of introducing children to Jamaica's signature rhythm. She is currently at work on her debut album, produced by her brothers Ziggy and Stephen.

Although there are great demands on her time as she juggles the aforementioned roles, Cedella's boundless creativity will not allow her to be limited to previous accomplishments. "I don't think I can ever reach a plateau where I'm like this is it, I don't have that type of personality," she says. "I'm always trying to do something else."

Cedella's parents, Bob and Rita, on their wedding day in February 1966. Cedella's life has always been rooted in music and culture. Growing up in Jamaica and touring the world as a Melody Maker, she had the best of both worlds—a little bit of country and a little rock 'n' roll.

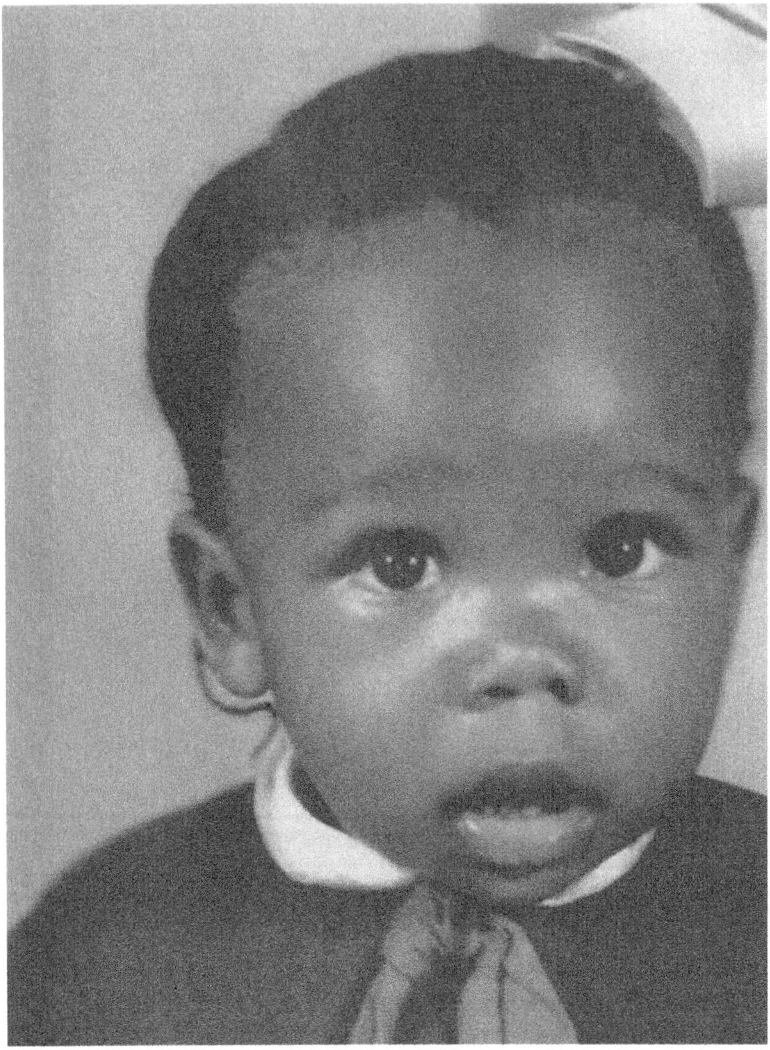

Cedella, age two. The Wailers celebrated Cedella's birth by writing and releasing the single "Nice Time," which later became her nickname. "Music was never a subject in our house . . . it was like food on the table," Cedella has said.

Cedella and family at their home in Kingston, Jamaica. This picture was taken during a photo shoot for Ziggy and the Melody Makers' second single entitled "Trodding." Bob Marley wrote the song for his family in 1975.

Cedella celebrating her eldest son's graduation from junior high school. From left to right: son Saiyan Marley Minto, son Skip Marley Minto, Cedella, husband David "Danny" Minto, and son Soul Rebel Marley.

A dramatic publicity still of Cedella in 1993. This was taken while promoting *Joey Breaker*, a full-length feature film starring Cedella with actors Richard Edson, Gina Gershon, and Fred Fondren.

Cedella with her namesake, paternal grandmother Cedella Marley Booker, in Orlando in 2000. Booker was also a musician and writer, releasing two music albums and two Bob Marley biographies, as well as collaborating artistically with her grandchildren.

Cedella with her sister Sharon (left) and mother Rita (right), celebrating Thanksgiving in 2009. Sharon, who resides in Jamaica, is a singer and dedicated supporter of charitable causes.

Cedella in a publicity photo by Peter Dean Richards. Like her older sister Sharon, Cedella is also active in many philanthropic projects including Africa Unite, Save the Children, charity: water, and the Bob Marley Foundation.

PHOTO CREDITS

All photos © Fifty-Six Hope Road Music, LTD.

The Man 1: Photo by Adrian Boot.
The Man 2: Photo by Adrian Boot.
The Man 3: Photo by Adrian Boot.
The Man 4: Photo by Adrian Boot.
The Man 5: Photo by Murphy/Hershman.
The Man 6: Photo by Dennis Morris.
The Man 7: Photo by Adrian Boot.
The Man 8: Photo by Adrian Boot.
The Man 9: Photo by Adrian Boot.
The Man 10: Photo by Adrian Boot.
The Man 11: Photo by Dennis Morris.
The Man 12: Photo by Dennis Morris.
The Man 13: Photo by Adrian Boot.
The Man 14: Photo by Adrian Boot.

The Music 1: Photo by Adrian Boot.
The Music 2: Photo by Adrian Boot.
The Music 3: Photo by Adrian Boot.
The Music 4: Photo by Adrian Boot.

The Music 5: Photo by Adrian Boot.
The Music 6: Photo by Adrian Boot.
The Music 7: Photo by Adrian Boot.
The Music 8: Photo by Murphy/Hershman.
The Music 9: Photo by Murphy/Hershman.
The Music 10: Photo by Dennis Morris.
The Music 11: Photo by Adrian Boot.
The Music 12: Photo by Adrian Boot.
The Music 13: Photo by Dennis Morris.
The Music 14: Photo by Dennis Morris.
The Music 15: Photo by Adrian Boot.

The Revolution 1: Photo by Adrian Boot.
The Revolution 2: Photo by Adrian Boot.
The Revolution 3: Photo by Adrian Boot.
The Revolution 4: Photo by Adrian Boot.
The Revolution 5: Photo by Adrian Boot.
The Revolution 6: Photo by Murphy/Hershman.
The Revolution 7: Photo by Dennis Morris.
The Revolution 8: Photo by Murphy/Hershman.
The Revolution 9: Photo by Adrian Boot.
The Revolution 10: Photo by Adrian Boot.
The Revolution 11: Photo by Adrian Boot.
The Revolution 12: Photo by Adrian Boot.
The Revolution 13: Photo by Adrian Boot.
The Revolution 14: Photo by Adrian Boot.

1LOVE.ORG

ONE LOVE. ONE HEART. ONE PURPOSE.

1Love.org is a movement with a simple mission: Do good in honor of Bob Marley's vision of hope and unity. Sparked by the Marley family, it's a flame that burns for youth, planet, and peace—supporting charities that empower people to take action for sustainable and responsible living, and encouraging acts of love and kindness that change the world little by little. We ask our community to help the flame burn brighter.

All rights reserved under International and Pan-American Copyright Conventions. By payment of the required fees, you have been granted the non-exclusive, non-transferable right to access and read the text of this book. No part of this text may be reproduced, transmitted, downloaded, decompiled, reverse engineered, or stored in or introduced into any information storage and retrieval system, in any form or by any means, whether electronic or mechanical, now known or hereinafter invented, without the express written permission of the publisher.

The Man:

Bob Marley biography written by Patricia Meschino

The Music:

56 Thoughts from 56 Hope Road: The Sayings & Psalms of Bob Marley
copyright © 2002 by Cedella Marley and Gerald Hausman
Lyrics courtesy of Blue Mountain Music Ltd/Irish Town Songs o/b/o Fifty-Six Hope Road Music Ltd and Blackwell Fuller Music Publishing LLC. Reprinted with permission. All rights reserved.

The Revolution:

60 Visions: A Book of Prophecy
copyright © 2004 by Cedella Marley and Gerald Hausman

Cover design by Andrea C. Uva

ISBN 978-1-4532-5476-9

This edition published in 2012 by Open Road Integrated Media
180 Varick Street
New York, NY 10014
www.openroadmedia.com

OPEN ROAD

INTEGRATED MEDIA

Videos, Archival Documents, and New Releases

Sign up for the Open Road Media newsletter and get news delivered straight to your inbox.

FOLLOW US:
@openroadmedia and
Facebook.com/OpenRoadMedia

SIGN UP NOW at
www.openroadmedia.com/newsletters

CPSIA information can be obtained
at www.ICGtesting.com
Printed in the USA
LVOW03s1037040218
565241LV00003B/633/P

9 781453 254769